ADD

W9-BJV-042

# Wedding
## SHOWERS

**CHICAGO PUBLIC LIBRARY**
**SOUTH CHICAGO BRANCH**
**9055 S. HOUSTON AVE.**
**CHICAGO, IL 60617**

# Wedding SHOWERS

CHICAGO PUBLIC LIBRARY
SOUTH CHICAGO BRANCH
9055 S. HOUSTON AVE.   60617

Jennifer Adams

Gibbs Smith, Publisher
Salt Lake City

First Edition
10 09 08 07 06  5 4 3 2 1

© 2006 by Jennifer Adams

All rights reserved. No part of this book may be reproduced by any means
whatsoever without written permission from the publisher, except brief
portions quoted for purpose of review.

Published by
Gibbs Smith, Publisher
P.O. Box 667
Layton, Utah 84041

Orders: 1.800.748.5439
www.gibbs-smith.com

Designed by Dawn DeVries Sokol
Cover artwork © CSAimages.com
Printed and bound in Korea

Library of Congress Cataloging-in-Publication Data

Adams, Jennifer.
  Wedding showers / Jennifer Adams.— 1st ed.
      p. cm.
  ISBN 1-58685-775-4
  1. Showers (Parties) 2. Weddings. I. Title.

GV147M.7.S5A316 2006
793.2—dc22

2005025798

SOC

$4.95

## DEDICATION

For my husband,
Virgil Grillone

CHICAGO PUBLIC LIBRARY
SOUTH CHICAGO BRANCH
9055 S. HOUSTON AVE. 60617

# Contents

# Acknowledgments

**Thank you** to Alison Koritz, Ankica Ostarcevic, Becky Oleson, Charlene Maynard, Darlene Roberts, Dayna Shoell, Dorothy Capson, Elizabeth McMullin, Janna DeVore, Jill Petty, Nancene Facer, Olga Grillone, Patrice Mealey, Shauna Larson, and Sheryl Smith for inspiring recipes and many lovely parties.

Thanks to Fred Przekop for sound advice on drinks and to Kellie Robles for collaborating with me on great places to get stationery, papers, and invitations. Special thanks to Madge Baird, an exceptional editor, and Suzanne Taylor, who does brilliant things with packaging and design.

Love and appreciation go to my family for helping me test the recipes included here. And special thanks to Aimee Stoddard and Melissa Jordan for editing, to Dawn DeVries Sokol for excellent design, and to all my friends at Gibbs Smith, Publisher.

# INTRODUCTION

The happy clatter of silver, the soft pinkness of rose petals, the rich taste of chocolate, the laughter of close friends. The gift of a wedding shower is the most personal and likely the most cherished gift you can give to someone who is getting married. The shower is not only a way to honor a person you care about, but also a chance to create a sense of celebration and intimacy, an opportunity to create treasured memories with family and friends that will last a lifetime.

## ○ ENJOY THE PLANNING ○

Planning a shower is half the fun! Enjoy organizing, brainstorming, and working with the bride to meet her needs and wants. Start by picking a date and making a list of the people you want to invite. Think about the different types of showers you might want to give. Do you want to throw a traditional shower or a more casual get-together? A Sunday brunch or an outdoor picnic? Soon a theme will emerge, giving you a general framework in which to plan for food, invitations, and decorations. The ideas will flow from there. Planning in advance obviously helps things go much more smoothly. Plan down to the details ahead of time and organize yourself with idea lists, shopping lists, and checklists.

## ○ KEEP PERSPECTIVE ○

A good friend of mine told me her mother made a wedding dress by hand when her sister got married. Her mom worked on it for six months. It was hand beaded and absolutely gorgeous. The morning of the wedding her mother was so stressed that when she got out the iron to do a last-minute pressing of the dress, she turned the heat too high. When she placed the hot iron on the front of the dress, she scorched it. The dress was ruined beyond repair.

After quite a few tears had been shed (by both sister and mother), my friend said that her sister was able to borrow a friend's wedding dress, and everyone went on to have a beautiful day. Compared to that dress fiasco—her mom losing six months of painstaking work and her sister losing the wedding dress her heart was set on wearing—most of the things that go wrong in planning an event are not so drastic. When you remember this, it's easier to be flexible in dealing with simple setbacks.

Of course, it's easier to relax and enjoy a party if there are no surprises, and the better you plan ahead of time, the less likely it is that there will be surprises. However, on the day of the shower, let yourself go with the flow. Sometimes things happen. Someone might break your crystal pitcher or spill cranberry juice on your white tablecloth. Your babysitter might cancel at the last minute or your really

**TIP:** Just decide to relax and have fun.

annoying aunt might show up even though she wasn't invited. Let it go! Just decide to relax and have fun. Remember, if you can relax and have a good time, so can your guests. I once gave a breakfast shower where the cinnamon rolls (the main part of the breakfast) didn't rise. Literally twenty minutes before the guests were to arrive,

I ran to the store and bought assorted fresh muffins. It didn't matter that we had store-bought muffins instead of homemade cinnamon rolls! There is a danger of getting so caught up in the details that if something goes wrong or differently than planned, you think the whole event is ruined. Keep things in perspective and allow yourself to deal with the changes. Remember that the event is a celebration and the point of it all is to honor the bride and have a good time.

## ○ GET ORGANIZED ○

It helps to make a master plan and timeline of what you want to accomplish. Most of your planning will be done in the six to eight weeks prior to the event. You can use the timeline that follows on pages 16 and 17 to help you.

Here are a couple of additional things to keep in mind:

Buy your gift for the bride early and stash it away; then you can wrap it when the day of the shower approaches. If you buy the gift in advance, then you spread out the cost of the shower. A danger of waiting until the last minute to buy the gift is that you'll be so overwhelmed with other preparations for food and decorations that you may not have the time or be able to savor choosing the perfect present. You'll also want to plan well in advance if your gift is handmade, such as a quilt or guest book for the wedding reception.

Planning ahead also holds true for the party favors. I've given showers where I didn't have favors because I waited until the last day to get them, and by that time I was out of time, energy, or money. While it's perfectly fine to do a shower without favors, it's a nice touch to have them and not much trouble if you plan for them in advance. If you are giving favors that can be made or bought ahead of time, buy them a month before and put them away for the shower. You could also keep a few things on hand, like candles or nice chocolate, that you could give away at a shower or in a variety of situations when a gift might be needed at the last minute.

Another way to make things simpler is to limit the number of people who help with the shower. Planning the event with a close friend is a great idea and you can have a lot of fun together. But be careful not to get too many people involved or else things may become disorganized. In many cases, especially with work showers, everyone will offer to help. Unless you want your shower to feel like a mismatched potluck, it's best to thank people graciously, but let them know you've got things covered. Otherwise, for example, you will

likely have people who are assigned food (a) come late, (b) come without their food made and want to use your kitchen to prepare it at the last minute, or (c) come with the wrong food that clashes with the menu you've planned. I've had all three happen.

## ○ TIMELINE ○

| | |
|---|---|
| *6 to 8 weeks before* | Talk to the bride about hosting a shower. Pick a date and location. Determine the guest list. |
| *6 weeks before* | Plan the menu and decorations. Buy or make the invitations. |
| *4 weeks before* | Buy your gift for the bride. Buy favors if not perishable. |
| *3 to 4 weeks before* | Send out invitations. Make sure you have the right linens, serving dishes, and so on. |

| | |
|---|---|
| *2 weeks before* | Deep clean your house and/or clean up your yard.<br>Order flowers.<br>Buy nonperishable food for the menu.<br>Buy or make other decorations. |
| *2 to 3 days before* | Do final cleaning. |
| *The day before*<br>*or the day of* | Buy perishable favors.<br>Buy perishable food for the menu.<br>Make the food.<br>Set up the decorations.<br>Pick up the flowers. |

# THEMES

Organizing a shower by theme gives you a framework in which to plan. Once you choose the theme, it tells you what colors to use, the style of the party, and even what food to serve. It makes the event feel like a cohesive whole. I once went to what was supposed to be a western-themed party where they served Chinese food—it was a bad combination. If you have a western party, have a barbecue. Serve barbecued chicken, baked beans, and homemade corn bread. If you have a luau, serve pork, rice, and tropical fruit salad.

Your shower theme often helps you decide who to invite. For example, a poolside shower might be a good way to accommodate couples; a lingerie shower works well for a smaller group of intimate friends. There are many themes you can choose from to organize your party. Be creative. Some favorites are included in this chapter.

## ◦ SEASONAL SHOWER ◦

Organizing by season is a simple and successful way to plan a wedding shower. When you coordinate a party  around a season, the right food for that season is available, there are decorations available in the right colors, and people are in the spirit. For example, a winter shower is a good time to decorate with garlands and greenery, and serve hot cocoa with peppermint and a sampling of cookies and bars. A fall shower lends itself to decorations and serving plates in a variety of autumn colors—burnt oranges, rich reds, browns, and earth tones. Serve soups and breads, and decorate with pumpkins or fall leaves. In spring, bright flowers are readily available, such as tulips and lilacs. It's a nice time for a light brunch of muffins and fresh fruit. Summer is the ideal season for an outdoor shower, a backyard barbecue, or a beach party. Grilled fish or chicken and favorite salads make a great menu.

## ◦ HOLIDAY SHOWER ◦

As with a seasonal shower, it's often fun to plan a shower around a holiday. Wedding showers are especially fun to plan around Valentine's Day. Heart-shaped cookies, pink punch, heart-shaped confetti, and pink and white flowers are easily worked into a Valentine's Day theme. You can buy invitations to match this theme as well, and at this time of year there are many heart-shaped and love-themed items that work perfectly as shower favors. Another favorite holiday is Christmas. If your home is already decorated for Christmas, very little additional work is needed to decorate for the shower. At this time of year, you'll find an abundance of invitations, decorations, plates, napkins, gifts, wrapping paper, and trinkets to tie into the Christmastime theme. Holiday showers around New Year's, the Fourth of July, Hanukkah, or other holidays that appeal to you are fun as well.

### ◦ AROUND-THE-CLOCK SHOWER ◦

For an around-the-clock shower, assign each guest a time on her invitation and tell her she should bring a gift that the bride would be able to use at that time of day. For example, if you are assigned 6:00 a.m., you might give a bathrobe; for 8:00 a.m., you might give a coffeemaker; for 8:00 p.m., a dressy handbag; or for 10:00 p.m., a set of sheets. Have the bride open the gifts in order, starting at the first morning hour you have assigned.

### ∘ PERSONAL SHOWER ∘

A personal shower is a favorite for many brides. For this type of shower, the gifts are centered around pampering the bride. Gift ideas include lingerie, lotions, bath salts, manicure sets, cozy slippers, a gift certificate for a massage, a basket of herbal teas, and so on.

### ∘ LINGERIE SHOWER ∘

The lingerie shower can be very nice. It's usually best with a group of personal friends rather than colleagues from work or the new mother-in-law's family. Some women like to do gag lingerie showers and give outrageous setups that most people would never use. (Envision pasties with bells and fruit leather underwear.)  A much more rewarding lingerie shower, for both the guests and the bride, is one where beautiful, tasteful lingerie is given. These showers are appreciated, as lingerie can be expensive and a shower like this gives the bride a nicer array of lingerie to start her marriage with than she'd be likely to splurge for on her own.

### ∘ SPA-DAY SHOWER ∘

Instead of planning a shower at your home, why not take a small group of guests for a day at the spa? Along with the bride, everyone can get a facial, pedicure, or massage. Go to someone's home or to your favorite coffee shop afterwards to enjoy a delicious dessert.

### ◦ OUT-TO-LUNCH SHOWER ◦

Sometimes rather than planning an elaborate meal at home, it's fun to take the bride to her favorite restaurant

for lunch. Reserve a table and enjoy the conversation and the food. This type of shower works best if the restaurant has a setting where all guests can be seated at one table and an ambiance where people can easily converse and enjoy the conversation without straining to hear what's being said. Have the bride open her gifts at the restaurant at the end of the lunch.

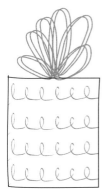

### ◦ GIRLS' SLEEPOVER SHOWER ◦

If you have a group of close college friends, or extended family who really like to spend time together, consider having a girls' sleepover. You might want to rent a condo, cabin, or weekend retreat, or just hang out at someone's house. Have everyone bring their pajamas, favorite treats,

## Great ROMANTIC Movies

*An Affair to Remember*

*The American President*

*Casablanca*

*Chocolat*

*Emma*

*The Englishman Who Went Up a Hill but Came Down a Mountain*

*Father of the Bride*

*Gigi*

*An Ideal Husband*

*The Importance of Being Earnest*

*It Happened One Night*

*The King and I*

*Moulin Rouge*

*My Best Friend's Wedding*

*My Big Fat Greek Wedding*

*Notting Hill*

*The Philadelphia Story*

*Pride and Prejudice*

*The Princess Bride*

*Random Harvest*

*Return to Me*

*Roman Holiday*

*Runaway Bride*

*Sabrina*

*Sense and Sensibility*

*Serendipity*

*Shakespeare in Love*

*Sleepless in Seattle*

*Sliding Doors*

*Strictly Ballroom*

*Two Weeks Notice*

*The Wedding Planner*

*When Harry Met Sally*

*While You Were Sleeping*

*You've Got Mail*

and favorite movies. After a night of classics like *Casablanca, Roman Holiday,* and *Pride and Prejudice,* or a round of chick flicks like *Sleepless*

*in Seattle, The Wedding Planner,* and *Runaway Bride,* even the most cynical among you will feel a twinge of unabashed romance about the upcoming wedding.

## ○ KITCHEN SHOWER ○

A kitchen shower is appropriate for the bride who has almost nothing for this room of the house. If you host a kitchen shower, it is best to tell guests where the bride is registered. Guests can give everything from utensils and mixing bowls to dishcloths and sets of china. For this type

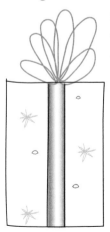

of shower, several guests often go in together to buy a larger gift, such as a food processor.

## ○ RECIPE SHOWER ○

The recipe shower is similar to the kitchen shower. Ask each guest to bring her favorite recipe to the shower and a gift that has something to do with that recipe. For example, for a recipe for chocolate cake, a guest might bring anything from chocolate, to the pan you bake the cake in, to the cake plate you serve it on. The bride ends up not only with nice presents, but with good recipes to add to her own collection.

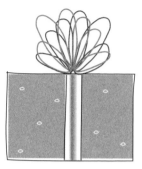

### ○ LINENS SHOWER

A linens shower is one of my favorites. For this shower, guests might bring towels, sheets, pillowcases, blankets, dishcloths, or even a bathrobe. You should let guests know where the bride is registered and what colors she would like for her bedroom, kitchen, and bath. The bride will get a surprising variety of gifts at this type of shower.

### ○ COUPLES SHOWER ○

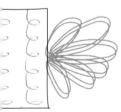

Traditionally showers have been exclusively for women, but many people now choose to host coed or couples showers. Just be sure to plan your event around the guest list. Men at a couples shower are more likely to enjoy a backyard barbecue than an afternoon tea with finger sandwiches and pound cake. Know your group, consider what they would enjoy, and plan accordingly.

Remember, when choosing a shower theme, keep foremost in your mind what the bride would like and enjoy. Tailor the shower to her as much as possible.

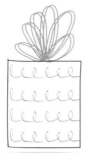

# INVITATIONS

What can be more fun than planning and putting together the invitations for a wedding shower? The invitation is a promise of what's to come. It sets the theme and creates the tone you want for the party. Will it be a large group, couples, or a few close friends? Will it be elegant, sassy, casual, or contemporary? You can browse your favorite stores, gift shops, or stationery stores for invitations to purchase or for ideas on making your own. Keep the bride in mind. By finding invitations that match her taste and style, you'll be on your way to determining the kind of shower you want to give. If you've already picked the theme for the shower, find invitations to reflect that theme.

## ○ WHOM TO INVITE ○

The invitations can be a good place to start on the shower planning. First you must draw up your guest list to figure out how many people you want to invite. This can be tricky. You want to invite the right size group. Clearly, you don't want to exclude anyone or hurt anyone's feelings. But you also don't want to invite people who aren't close to the bride or who don't know any of the other guests. For one shower I planned for a colleague at work, I spent a good deal of time mulling over whom to invite. I finally settled on all the women in my department. This seemed a clear dividing line, and inviting everyone in the office would have both made the shower too large and included people the bride didn't really have interaction with. However, when people started talking about the shower at work, one woman's feelings were really hurt that she wasn't included. In some cases it's better to invite a few more people than to risk hurt feelings.

On the other hand, always work toward creating a group for the shower that makes sense—one where the people will get along well and that is the right size. Most brides will have more than one shower, based on groups of family, friends, and coworkers, so guest lists can overlap. Having the bride help you draw up the list will eliminate problems and help you figure out whom to include. And always remember that a shower is meant to be an intimate event to celebrate the wedding—smaller showers are often more successful than ones that get too big.

## ◦ CHOOSING THE INVITATION ◦

A beautiful, "inviting" invitation can get guests excited for your event and hint at what is to come. You can spend a little or quite a lot of money on invitations. Figure out your budget and work from there. Many people create beautiful handmade invitations for very little cost. You can find papers, card stocks, and vellum sheets in a multitude of colors, patterns, textures, and styles. Home printers can print on most papers with a variety of fonts. You can use handmade paper, print on an overlay vellum sheet, do hand lettering, or combine papers in many different ways to create the style of invitation you want. Adding a delicate ribbon or a tiny line of beads can be just the right detail to make the invitation complete.

For purchased invitations, you can hand letter them, print them on your computer, or have the stationery shop print them for you. Letterpress printed invitations can be whimsical to exquisite; they give an added sense that something special is being celebrated. Following is a list

of favorite stationery stores and invitation lines. There are some really beautiful and creative things to choose from. Some of these invitations and papers can be purchased online. In most cases, the website will direct you to the store nearest you that carries the line of stationery you are interested in.

## Invitation RESOURCES

**GENERAL**

Crane
www.crane.com

Kate's Paperie
www.katespaperie.com

Max and Lucy
www.maxandlucy.com

Papyrus
www.papyrusonline.com

Snow and Graham
www.snowandgraham.com

William Arthur
www.williamarthur.com

**LETTERPRESS**

Claudia Calhoun
www.claudiacalhoun.com

Elum
www.elumdesigns.com

Julie Holcomb Printers
www.julieholcombprinters.com

Oblation Papers and Press
www.oblationpapers.com

**HANDMADE PAPERS**

Renaissance Writings
www.rwinvite.com

## ○ INFORMATION TO INCLUDE ○

Be sure to include the following information on your invitation:

What
For Whom
When
Where
RSVP

**TIP:** A shower theme or where the bride is registered can be incorporated into the invitation as well.

For example:

Please join us for a bridal shower
honoring

Anne Florian

Saturday, October 25
11:00 a.m.

174 West 42nd Street
New York

**TIP:** Maps or directions to the shower location can be included on separate inserts.

RSVP
Maria Hunter
874.4228

# DECORATIONS

Decorations, from the simple to the elaborate, can transform a regular setting into a place of celebration. Who doesn't love to enter a home that has been bedecked with fresh-cut flowers, twinkling lights, clever centerpieces, or candles? To decorate for a wedding shower you can use cut flowers, balloons, Christmas lights, canopies, banners, holiday decorations, baskets of fruit or other fresh produce, luminaries, topiaries, wreaths, trellises, confetti, candles, and even fireworks like sprinklers or fountains to set the scene and create a feeling of joy, celebration, and fun.

Do as little or as much as you wish by way of decorating, but remember that less is often more, and a few nicely placed touches often achieve the same desired effect as an elaborate overhaul of a room.

## ❀ FRESH-CUT FLOWERS ❀

The absolute best decorations you can provide for a wedding shower are fresh flowers. Fresh-cut flowers say romance like almost nothing else and show that the event is something special that you were willing to splurge on. If you have a beautiful centerpiece of flowers, more decorations really aren't necessary unless you want them.

You may want to choose the flowers based on the bride's wedding colors, or simply use the bride's favorite flowers. One nice option is to ask the bride what flowers she has chosen for her wedding bouquet and then make an arrangement incorporating those flowers for the shower. This gives guests a preview of the wedding flowers and ties in the shower with the wedding reception.

TIP: Put some time into arranging flowers.

Many people already have a favorite florist whose style they trust. If you don't have a florist, start noticing flower arrangements that you like—at restaurants, other parties, weddings, and so on. Ask around to find out who the florist is.

You can also buy flowers rather inexpensively at farmers markets or green grocers. Costco and other price clubs often sell fresh flowers at very affordable prices. Even grocery

# TIPS ON FLOWER ARRANGING

- *Recut the stems so the flowers have a fresh cut to soak up the water. Cut at an angle to allow more surface for water absorption.*

- *Put flowers in an unusual container, such as a tall square vase, a flat round bowl, or a ceramic pitcher.*

- *Add pretty greenery, such as lemon leaves or eucalyptus.*

- *Use odd numbers of your main flower; for example, seven lilies, roses, or dahlias will usually look better than six in an arrangement.*

- *If you buy roses at the grocery store, throw away the baby's breath and add a different filler. Baby's breath often looks tired and is expected. Change the arrangement to something unexpected by adding fresh chiles, pine boughs, or coffee beans.*

- *Play with different stem lengths. Cut some stems shorter than others.*

- *Add cut branches, corkscrew willows, pussy tails, or other tall "sticks" to give height and proportion to your arrangement.*

- *Use different colors to complement and contrast.*

- *Incorporate fresh fruit if possible. For example, make an arrangement with green apples and green hydrangeas, or fill the bottom of your clear vase with fresh cranberries.*

- *Tie the vase with ribbon. Ribbons can distinctly change the look of an arrangement. For example, use gingham for a more casual feel, netting ribbon for a lighter and more romantic look, or silk to add a touch of elegance. You can bring out the colors and style of your arrangement by the type of ribbon you select.*

stores sell a dozen roses for under ten dollars. And don't forget the option of raiding your (or your mother's or friend's) yard or garden.

When you buy flowers to arrange yourself rather than getting them from a florist, the key is putting some time into arranging them. Don't just shove them in a vase when you get home.

## ○ FLOWERS BY SEASON ○

Often the season dictates what flowers to use.

In spring, you can cut branches from blossoming apple or apricot trees. Arranged in a tall vase, they make breathtaking centerpieces. Or use fresh spring flowers from your garden or local florist—tulips, daffodils, and iris are in abundance at this time of year. Bouquets of fresh lilacs cut from your yard are fragrant as well as beautiful. Freesia in a pot with a little moss at the base makes a delicate centerpiece.

In summer, bright flowers are often best. Use burnt orange roses, bright red and fuchsia gerbera daisies, or yellow calla lilies with dark greenery. A simple bouquet of fresh daisies gives a cheerful ambiance to a room. A

**TIP:** Bright flowers are often best in summer.

floating gardenia in a clear glass bowl makes an elegant centerpiece.

In fall, gather fresh bouquets and put in vases or tie to the backs of chairs for a luncheon. Use cut branches with berries, such as pyracantha, or autumn leaves. Wild sunflowers make excellent bouquets in late summer and early fall. Chrysanthemums are in abundance at this time of year and come in many shades of fall colors.

In winter, garlands are an obvious choice. Pine boughs draped with white lights are beautiful and can be whimsical. Use baskets of pinecones spiced with cinnamon oil. Bunches of poinsettias can be grouped as decorations around the room—then can be sent home with guests as party favors. Fragrant white lilies mix well with red roses and dark greenery at this time of year. A big bouquet of holly with red berries is an unexpected and delightful centerpiece at Christmastime.

Stargazer lilies are bold and beautiful flowers in arrangements at any time of the year, especially if your bride is having a pink wedding. Roses are, of course, the favorite standby. Besides being beautiful, roses come in almost any color imaginable and hold up for nearly a week. Mix roses with different flowers to make beautiful arrangements. Remember that white flowers

# FLOWERS by Cost

| _Inexpensive_ | _Season_ | _Color_ |
|---|---|---|
| Daffodil | spring | yellow |
| Dahlia | fall | pink, purple, red, yellow, white |
| Daisy | year-round | white with yellow center |
| Delphinium | year-round | dark blue, light blue, white |
| Freesia | year-round | purple, yellow, orange, hot pink, white |
| Gerbera Daisy | year-round | yellow, orange, red, pink, white |
| Iris | year-round | yellow, purple |
| Ranunculus | spring | pink, hot pink, orange, red, yellow, white |
| Snapdragon | year-round | pink, burgundy, yellow, orange, white |
| Stock | year-round | white, purple, pink, peach |
| Sunflower | fall | yellow |
| Sweet Pea | spring | pink, peach, lavender, burgundy, white |

| *Medium Cost* | *Season* | *Color* |
| --- | --- | --- |
| Amaryllis | winter | red, white, pink, orange |
| Hyacinth | spring | pink, dark purple, white |
| Rose | year-round | all colors |
| Tulip | spring | pink, red, white, yellow, orange |

---

| *Expensive* | *Season* | *Color* |
| --- | --- | --- |
| Bird-of-Paradise | winter | orange |
| Calla Lily | year-round | white, yellow, peach, burgundy |
| Gardenia | year-round | white |
| Hydrangea | summer | pink, blue, green, burgundy |
| Orchid | year-round | all colors |
| Stargazer Lily | year-round | deep pink, white |

are always a good choice for wedding showers. There are many different shades of white that you can combine in arrangements for beautiful bouquets.

**TIP:** White flowers are always a good choice.

**NOTE:** Avoid carnations—they are rather inelegant and are associated with cheap restaurants and plastic tablecloths.

## ◦ ADDITIONAL DECORATIONS ◦

In addition to a floral centerpiece, there are other simple decorations you can use to dress up a shower.

White Christmas lights on the house or along railings look magical on snowy days. They are also very pleasant used on an outdoor canopy or deck on summer evenings.

Make luminaries by putting small white votive candles in cans or small paper bags. You can weigh down the bags with sand or dry beans. Use them to line the walkway leading to your door.

Tie a big bouquet of balloons to the porch or railing as a nice indicator of where the shower is. It's especially helpful if you're having guests who haven't been to your home before. Send the balloon bouquet home with the bride.

Adorn banisters with ribbon, garlands, flowers, or lights.

**NOTE:** Don't use crepe paper—it looks and feels cheap.

# GAMES

My number one recommendation about games at a wedding shower is *don't* have them. When you talk to people in their candid moments, you'll find that most really dread shower games. It's usually so much more fun and meaningful to sit and talk with friends, listen to stories of everyone's experiences, and hear the bride's future plans. Visiting over the food and then opening presents takes ample time; games are not necessary.

However, some people do enjoy shower games, and games can be fun icebreakers at parties where the guests might not know each other well. Here are a few favorite games you can try.

## ○ KITCHEN EQUIPMENT ○

For a younger bride who doesn't already have her house set up, buy a supply of kitchen items and utensils—about twenty or so. For example, measuring cups, spatula, pancake turner, baster, pastry brush, cheese grater, ice-cream scoop, and so on. Arrange all the items on a tray. Give each woman a piece of paper and a pencil. Then bring out the tray and let guests look at the items for about sixty seconds. Take away the tray or cover it with a cloth. Guests now have another sixty seconds to write down all the items they remember. The person with the most correct items wins. Be sure to provide a prize.

## ○ STOCK THE PANTRY ○

This game is similar to the Kitchen Equipment game. Buy a couple bags of groceries—the basics like flour, sugar, pasta, ketchup, mustard, mayonnaise, pancake mix, syrup, or other nonperishables. Set everything in the center of the room and give everyone a few minutes to calculate the price of all the groceries + tax (remember to keep your receipt for reference). The person who guesses closest to the total cost of the items gets a prize and the bride takes the groceries home.

### ◦ SHARE ADMIRATION ◦

A simple but often meaningful activity for a wedding shower is to go around the room and let each person tell one thing she admires about the bride.

### ◦ GIVE ADVICE ◦

Along the same lines, you can go around the room and have each guest give one piece of advice to the bride. A list of some sage tidbits follows on page 48.

### ◦ DESIGN A WEDDING DRESS ◦

The toilet paper wedding dress is a classic bridal shower game, if a little bit wacky. It's a fun game to use for younger guests. (Great-Aunt Matilda probably won't enjoy being wrapped in toilet paper.) Divide guests into two or three teams, depending on the number of guests. The bride is the moderator. Have each team pick a model. Give each team two to three rolls of toilet paper, a stapler, and a roll of scotch tape. The bride starts a timer, and the teams have ten minutes to design and decorate their model in a toilet-paper bridal gown, complete with veil if they like. The bride chooses a winner, or you can

**TIP:** This game is best for younger guests.

## WEDDING SHOWER ADVICE

- *Realize that there are days he's really going to bother you.*

- *Happiness is a choice.*

- *Those who say you should never go to bed angry at each other are either very young or very tired.*

- *Marriage is hard work.*

- *Indulge him sometimes.*

- *Forgive.*

- *Sometimes you should just laugh about it—it's better than crying.*

- *Don't argue in bed.*

- *Surprise is an element of romance.*

- *Remember to dress up and go out.*

- *Let it go.*

- *Never say you can't afford to buy each other gifts.*

- *Start your own traditions.*

- *Even the best in-laws are in-laws.*

- *A compromise is when neither person gets what they want. Marriage is full of compromises.*

- *Keep "please" and "thank you" as part of your vocabulary.*

- *Don't give up the simple pleasure of holding hands.*

- *Remember why you married him.*

have a prize for each dress, such as most romantic, most sexy, most creative, and most elaborate. Even though this game isn't a favorite of mine, I have to admit that I've seen some fun designs.

### ◦ GETTING TO KNOW YOU ◦

In advance of the shower, make a quiz about the bride. Ask her about her favorites, from movie, to song, to class in college, to candy bar. Include other questions, such as who was the first boy she kissed or what was her most embarrassing moment. Make a list of about twenty questions and keep her answers on a separate paper. At the shower, give the quiz. The guest who "knows the bride best," or gets the most correct answers, wins. This is fun at a party with close family members where everyone thinks she knows the bride best. People can get competitive when they don't get all the answers right.

You can also make a quiz about the bride's fiancé and then test the bride at the shower. Don't let her know you are planning this, but call her fiancé and get his answers ahead of time. Include questions such as what was his mother's maiden name, where was he born, or what is his favorite food, sports team, vacation spot, and so on. Try to include some questions that you don't think the bride will know. At the shower give her the quiz in front of everyone. Then have the groom make a guest appearance while you correct her answers!

## ○ LOVE POETRY ○

Pass out favorite love poems or sonnets and take turns reading them aloud. Or you can hold a competition to write a love poem. Divide guests into two groups (excluding the bride) and provide a list of words that must be used in the poems. Give a time limit. Someone from each group then reads her group's poem. The bride is the judge of which poem is best. A variation is to write the poem as a group. The bride writes the first line. Then she passes it to the person sitting next to her, who adds the next line. The poem is passed all the way around the room, with each person adding just one line. When it makes its way back to the bride again, she reads the completed poem aloud to everyone.

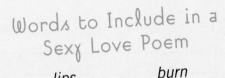

## Words to Include in a Sexy Love Poem

lips

eyes

breath

burn

desire

passion

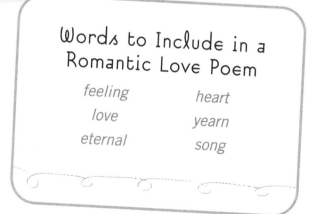

## Words to Include in a Romantic Love Poem

feeling

love

eternal

heart

yearn

song

# RECIPES

Showers lend themselves well to finger foods and dainty appetizers, salads, light lunches, mid-morning brunches, or just lovely desserts. The following recipes were chosen for their taste, presentation, ease of preparation, and appeal. You can use these recipes separately, combine them into menus, or add your own favorite recipes to create the perfect menu.

## ◦ CHOOSING INGREDIENTS ◦

When shopping for fresh produce and baked goods, it is best to buy them the day of the shower or the day before, if possible, to ensure freshness. Farmers markets and green grocers are often the best places to get ripe, organic, beautiful fruits and vegetables. Even if you don't shop there regularly, consider doing so when cooking for a party. Also keep in mind with the recipes included here, as with any, you do not have to be a stickler for every specific ingredient. If your vegetarian quiche calls for fresh mushrooms and the mushrooms at the store look shriveled, leave them out of the recipe, or substitute them with sliced zucchini. If you were planning on making a fresh salsa but the tomatoes look unripe, then consider changing to a mango and black bean salsa. Pay attention to the ingredients and never force a menu if the ingredients won't live up to it—otherwise the food will suffer.

**TIP:** Consider shopping at farmers markets and green grocers for the best produce.

## ◦ A WORD ABOUT PRESENTATION ◦

When I was about eight years old, I made my first meal for my family all by myself. I made macaroni and cheese, creamed corn, and canned pears. When I proudly set a

## GARNISHES

*Here is a list of garnishes to keep in mind. Their addition to the right dish can change it from something good to something fabulous.*

- *Fresh mint sprigs*
- *Fresh rosemary sprigs*
- *Drizzled chocolate syrup*
- *Drizzled caramel syrup*
- *Drizzled raspberry syrup*
- *Curled orange peel shavings*
- *Chocolate shavings (white chocolate or dark chocolate)*
- *Fresh strawberries (make sure they are very red and ripe), whole or sliced*
- *Fresh lime slices*
- *Kiwifruit slices*
- *Sprinkled powdered sugar*
- *Chocolate sprinkles or miniature chocolate chips*
- *Coconut (toasted or untoasted)*
- *Fresh raspberries, blueberries, or boysenberries (or a mixture of these)*
- *Toasted, sliced, or slivered almonds*
- *Chopped walnuts or other nuts*
- *Pomegranate seeds*
- *Pirouette cookie straws*
- *Whole cinnamon sticks*
- *Fresh currants (if you can find them)*
- *Nonpareils*

plate before my mom, she made a noise that sounded very close to "ugh." That was my introduction to the importance of color—you *must* have contrast—and presentation with food.

I've since learned, through more pleasant experiences, that presentation can be nine-tenths of the success of a dish. The value of a beautiful garnish can't be overstated. A layered chocolate cake is a layered chocolate cake, but a layered chocolate cake topped with hand-carved chocolate shavings and fresh raspberries is something to "ahh" over. A simple slice of key lime pie can be dressed up by drizzling raspberry syrup in a zigzag pattern over a white plate, sprinkling the pie with powdered sugar, and adding a dollop of whipped cream, a slice of kiwifruit, and a strawberry on top. That's the difference between a piece of pie that's not long remembered and a dessert at your favorite restaurant for which you pay five dollars. It's all in the presentation.

## ✳ APPETIZERS ✳

These appetizers can be combined in different ways to make a lovely buffet or can be served with the lunch recipes from later in this chapter.

## MELON WITH FETA AND PINE NUTS

6 cups watermelon chunks

½ small red onion, minced

¼ cup chopped fresh mint leaves plus leaves for garnish

1 tablespoon fresh lime juice

½ teaspoon freshly ground pepper

½ cup crumbled feta cheese

¼ cup toasted pine nuts

Put melon, onion, mint, lime juice, and pepper in a bowl and toss to mix well. Top with feta cheese and pine nuts. Chill until time to serve. Garnish with mint leaves.

------------------------------------

Makes 8 servings

# Chocolate-Dipped Strawberries

1 pound fresh strawberries with leaves
16 ounces semisweet chocolate chips
2 tablespoons shortening

Wash strawberries and dry on paper towels. Insert toothpicks into the tops of the strawberries.

In a double boiler, melt the chocolate and shortening, stirring occasionally until the mixture is smooth. Holding each strawberry by the toothpick, dip it into the chocolate mixture until it is three-fourths submerged. Place on wax paper and let the chocolate cool and harden.

------------------------------------------------------------------------

Makes about 8 servings of 2 strawberries each

**VARIATION:** *Use white chocolate chips instead of semisweet chocolate chips. Or you can melt white chocolate chips separately and drizzle over the strawberries dipped in semisweet chocolate.*

# BAKED BRIE

1 package puff pastry sheets
1 egg
1 tablespoon water
1 15-ounce wheel brie
red grapes for garnish

Preheat oven to 350 degrees. Thaw pastry sheets at
room temperature. Make an egg wash by combining egg
and water. Open and flatten pastry. Place brie in the
center, and wrap pastry to cover brie. Cut off excess
pastry dough and form the loose ends of the dough
together to make a seam. Seal seam with egg wash.
Place seam side down on a baking sheet. Brush top and
sides with egg wash and bake 20 minutes or until pastry is golden brown. Let stand for 1 hour before serving.
Serve with clusters of red grapes.

Makes 8 servings

**NOTE:** *You can cut out shapes, such as leaves or flowers, with the*
*excess dough and place on top of the pastry-wrapped brie before*
*baking. You can also cut the pastry dough into strips and make a*
*woven pattern over the brie instead of wrapping it completely.*

# CHICKEN CAESAR SALAD SQUARES

Pillsbury pizza crust
3 chicken breasts, cooked
½ cup grated fresh Parmesan
    cheese, divided
½ cup Caesar salad dressing
1 teaspoon lemon pepper

½ garlic clove, minced
1 8-ounce package cream cheese
4 cups thinly sliced romaine
    lettuce
1 small can sliced black olives,
    drained

Bake pizza crust on a baking sheet according to package directions. Finely chop half the chicken; slice remaining chicken into strips. Set chicken aside. In a small bowl, combine ¼ cup Parmesan cheese, salad dressing, lemon pepper, and garlic. Mix together.

In a separate bowl, mix cream cheese, half of the dressing mixture you've just made, and the chopped chicken. Toss together remaining dressing mixture, lettuce, and olives.

Spread cream cheese mixture evenly over the baked crust. Sprinkle lettuce mixture on top. Arrange the sliced chicken pieces on top of this and sprinkle with remaining Parmesan. Cut into squares.

Makes 12 servings

# BRUSCHETTA

**For Pesto:**

1 cup extra-virgin olive oil

1 large garlic clove, minced

10 to 12 fresh basil leaves, minced

½ to 1 bunch parsley, minced

**For Bruschetta:**

sourdough french baguette

olive oil

1 small jar marinated artichoke
hearts, finely chopped

8 ounces mozzarella cheese,
grated

¾ cup finely grated Parmesan
cheese

To make pesto, combine olive oil, garlic, basil, and parsley. Mix together. This can be stored in the refrigerator in a jar with a tight lid for up to 3 weeks.

To make bruschetta, slice baguette in ¾-inch-thick slices. Place slices on a baking sheet and broil until lightly toasted. Drizzle each slice with olive oil. Top each slice with chopped artichokes, then a thin layer of mozzarella cheese, and then a thin layer of pesto.

Broil bruschetta on high until cheese is melted. Remove from oven and sprinkle with Parmesan cheese.

----------------------------------

Makes 12 servings

## ❋ BRUNCHES ❋

Brunches make a nice, light meal for a bridal shower. Serve muffins or quiche with fruit kebobs and dip. Crepes make a lovely brunch on their own. Or you can serve a combination of breads, rolls, and fruit in a buffet-style menu.

## RED-AND-BLUE FRUIT KEBOBS

2 pints fresh strawberries
1 pint fresh blueberries
8 skewers

Wash fruit and remove stems from strawberries. Cut large strawberries in half lengthwise. Smaller strawberries can stay whole. Thread 2 strawberries, then 2 blueberries, then 2 strawberries, then 2 blueberries on each skewer. Arrange on a platter or serving plate.

---------------------------------

Makes 8 servings

*Serve with Lemon-Yogurt Fruit Dip (see recipe on page 68).*

# APPLE-CINNAMON MUFFINS

3 cups peeled and finely
   chopped apples
1 cup sugar
1 cup brown sugar
1 cup vegetable oil
3 eggs

2 teaspoons vanilla
1 tablespoon cinnamon
3½ cups flour
1 teaspoon salt
2 teaspoons baking soda
cinnamon and sugar for topping

Preheat oven to 350 degrees. Grease and flour muffin tins or use paper liners. Thoroughly combine apples and sugars. Add oil, eggs, and vanilla. Sift together cinnamon, flour, salt, and soda; then mix into the apple mixture. The batter will be very thick and gooey. Fill muffin tins two-thirds full; sprinkle with cinnamon-and-sugar mixture. Bake about 30 minutes.

-----------------------------------

Makes 12 muffins

# Blueberry Streusel Muffins

**For Muffins:**

½ cup sugar

¼ cup butter, softened

1 egg, beaten

2⅓ cups flour

4 teaspoons baking powder

½ teaspoon salt

1 cup milk

1 teaspoon vanilla

1½ cups fresh blueberries

**For Streusel:**

½ cup sugar

⅓ cup flour

½ teaspoon cinnamon

¼ cup butter

In a mixing bowl, cream sugar and butter. Add egg; mix well.

Combine flour, baking powder, and salt. Add to the butter mixture alternately with milk. Stir in vanilla. Do not overmix. Gently fold in blueberries.

Grease and flour a large 6-muffin tin or regular 12-muffin tin. Fill cups two-thirds full.

To make streusel, in a small bowl combine sugar, flour, and cinnamon; cut in butter until crumbly. Sprinkle over muffin batter. Bake at 375 degrees for 25 to 30 minutes or until browned.

---

Makes 6 large or 12 regular muffins

## Banana Bread

1 cup sugar
½ cup shortening
2 eggs
2 cups flour
1 teaspoon baking soda
3 soft, ripe bananas, mashed
½ cup chopped pecans (optional)

Preheat oven to 325 degrees. Cream together sugar and shortening. Add eggs, flour, soda, bananas, and nuts if using. Pour batter into a greased and floured loaf pan. Bake for about 1 hour and 15 minutes, or until a toothpick inserted in center comes out clean.

--------------------------------
Makes 12 slices

# Orange Rolls

**For Rolls:**

1 medium orange rind, grated

½ cup sugar

12 frozen Rhodes Texas Rolls, thawed but still cold

¼ cup butter, melted

**For Glaze:**

1 cup powdered sugar

1 tablespoon butter, melted

3 tablespoons orange juice

½ teaspoon vanilla

To make rolls, in a small bowl mix orange rind with sugar and set aside. Roll each roll into a 9-inch rope. Tie each rope in a loose knot. Roll each knot in melted butter and then roll in sugar mixture. Place on baking sheet sprayed with nonstick cooking spray. Cover with plastic wrap and let rise until double in size.

Remove plastic wrap and bake at 350 degrees for 15 to 20 minutes. Remove rolls from pan and place on a cooling rack.

For citrus glaze, combine sugar, butter, orange juice, and vanilla. Brush rolls with glaze while still warm.

Makes 12 rolls

# Lemon-Yogurt Fruit Dip

1 8-ounce carton lemon yogurt

1 8-ounce carton sour cream

1 to 2 tablespoons powdered sugar

1 tablespoon fresh grated lemon rind

Combine all ingredients until well blended. Refrigerate for 1 hour before serving.

------------------------------------

Makes 2 cups

# TROPICAL FRUIT SALAD

1 papaya, peeled, seeded, and sliced

1 cup fresh pineapple chunks

2 kiwifruits, peeled and sliced

1 cup watermelon balls

1 pint strawberries

juice of 1 lime

mint sprigs for garnish (optional)

Place fruit in a serving bowl. Cover with lime juice and toss lightly to coat. Garnish with mint sprigs, if desired.

--------------------------------

Makes 8 servings

# CHEESE AND ONION QUICHE

For Crust:

33 soda crackers, rolled into crumbs

6 tablespoons butter, melted

For Filling:

1 bunch green onions, sliced

4 tablespoons butter

4 eggs, beaten

¾ cup sour cream

2½ cups grated swiss cheese

½ teaspoon salt

1 to several dashes cayenne pepper (to taste)

Combine cracker crumbs and butter to make crust. Press into the bottom of a 9-inch pie plate.

For filling, sauté onion in butter until soft. Spread onion onto crumb crust.

Mix together well eggs, sour cream, cheese, salt, and cayenne pepper. Pour mixture into crust. Bake at 350 degrees for 40 minutes or until center is slightly puffed. If ingredients are cold when combined, bake a little longer.

--------------------------------

Makes 8 servings

**VARIATION:** *Add ½ cup diced ham.*

# POTATO CROQUETTES

4 cups cooked, mashed potatoes

2 eggs, lightly beaten

2 to 4 tablespoons buttermilk

3 tablespoons chopped fresh
    chives

1 teaspoon salt

¼ teaspoon white pepper

1½ cups crushed Ritz cracker
    crumbs (about 40 crackers)

½ teaspoon paprika

¼ cup grated Parmesan cheese

Combine mashed potatoes, eggs, buttermilk, chives, salt, and pepper in a bowl. Divide mixture into 12 to 16 small balls.

In a separate bowl, combine cracker crumbs, paprika, and Parmesan. Roll balls in crumbs. Place croquettes on a lightly greased baking sheet and bake at 350 degrees for 15 minutes or until golden brown. Or, alternately, deep-fry in oil and drain on paper towels.

Makes 6 to 8 servings

# CREPES

**For Batter:**

3 eggs

1 egg yolk

¾ teaspoon salt

1½ cups milk

½ cup water

5 tablespoons butter, melted

1 tablespoon oil

1¼ cups flour

**For Filling and Topping:**

4 cups fresh raspberries
(thawed frozen raspberries
may also be used)

sweetened whipping cream

raspberry syrup for garnish

To make batter, combine eggs, egg yolk, salt, milk, water, butter, oil, and flour. Blend until batter is smooth and thin.

Heat a crepe pan or small skillet over medium heat. Lightly butter pan; pour in about ⅛ cup batter. Rotate pan to cover the bottom with batter. Place over heat. When edges are lightly brown, flip crepe over with a pancake turner to cook the other side. Place finished crepes in a baking dish, separated with wax paper, and keep warm in oven.

To assemble, place a crepe on a plate and put about ½ cup fresh berries down the center. Top with a couple of dollops of whipped cream. Fold the sides over the top of each other, and then place the crepe seam side down on the serving plate. Top with another dollop of whipped cream and drizzle with raspberry syrup.

**VARIATION:** *Substitute 4 cups of fresh sliced peaches for the berries. Drizzle with apricot syrup instead of raspberry syrup.*

Makes 8 crepes

## For an Easy Fix

- *Serve Pillsbury orange rolls. They are almost as good as homemade and only take 8 minutes to bake. Buy in the refrigerated section of the grocery store.*

- *Buy an assortment of fresh pastries at your favorite bakery.*

- *Buy a fruit plate already cut up at the grocery store and then thread fruit kebobs on skewers yourself. This saves you time as well as the messy task of washing and chopping all the fruit.*

## ✳ LUNCHES ✳

The following recipes for salads and soups make excellent light lunches. Serve the soups with baguette, croissants, rolls, or french bread. The salads also make a nice evening supper when combined with a dessert from the recipes later in this chapter. Other recipes are included here for more substantial lunches; these work well for evening dinner showers too.

## CLASSIC CHICKEN SALAD

6 double chicken breasts

2 cups mayonnaise

juice of 2 lemons

1 celery stalk, diced

1 bunch green onions, sliced

1 cup cashews

2 cups red seedless grapes

lettuce leaves for serving

black olives or fresh strawberries for garnish (optional)

--------------------------------------------------------------------------

Preheat oven to 350 degrees. Salt the chicken breasts, cover with foil, and bake in a glass dish for 40 minutes. Be careful not to overbake or chicken will be too dry. When cooked, put chicken in fridge to cool; when it is cool enough to handle, cut into small cubes.

In a large bowl, make dressing by combining mayonnaise, lemon juice, celery, and onion. Add more lemon juice if dressing is too thick. Add chicken and mix well. Chill for 3 to 4 hours to let flavors blend.

Right before serving, fold in nuts and grapes. Serve on a plate with a lettuce leaf. Garnish with black olives or fresh strawberries, if desired.

------------------------------------------

Makes 12 to 15 servings

**VARIATION:** *Serve on croissants to make chicken salad sandwiches.*

# CRAB AND SWISS MELT

6 slices french bread
1 cup crabmeat, flaked
1¼ cup diced swiss cheese
1 green onion, minced
¼ cup mayonnaise
1 tablespoon lemon juice
salt and pepper to taste

Cut 6 slices from a loaf of french bread, about ½ inch to ⅜ inch thick each. Place slices on a baking sheet and broil until lightly toasted. Turn and toast the other side. Take baking sheet from oven and set aside.

In a bowl, combine crabmeat, cheese, onion, mayonnaise, lemon juice, and salt and pepper. Divide the mixture between the slices of bread. Return baking sheet to oven and broil until cheese melts.

----------------------------------

Makes 6 servings

# MANDARIN CHICKEN SALAD

4 boneless, skinless chicken
  breasts
2 cups Oriental salad dressing
1 cup fried wonton strips
oil for deep-frying
2 heads green leaf lettuce

2 11-ounce cans mandarin
  oranges, drained
1 cup pea pods, ends removed
1 red bell pepper, cut in strips
4 green onions, sliced

Marinate chicken in 1 cup Oriental salad dressing for
4 hours. Remove from marinade and grill chicken on an
outside grill so it has crosshatch grill marks. Cut into
strips. Discard marinade.

Cut wonton wrappers into strips and deep-fry in hot oil.
Drain on paper towels. Wash lettuce and pat dry with
paper towels; tear into bite-sized pieces. Combine
lettuce, chicken, mandarin oranges, pea pods, red bell
pepper, and green onions in a large bowl. Pour remaining
dressing over salad; toss to coat evenly. Top with wonton
strips and serve.

Makes 8 main dish servings

# Almond Craisin Salad

**For Salad:**

1 head red leaf lettuce

1 head green leaf lettuce

1 head romaine lettuce

8 ounces finely grated
   mozzarella cheese

1 6-ounce package grated
   Parmesan cheese

1 package craisins

1 package bacon, cooked and
   crumbled

1 6-ounce package sliced
   almonds

4 to 6 chicken breasts, grilled
   and diced (optional)

**For Dressing:**

½ cup chopped red onion

1 cup sugar

1½ teaspoons salt

2 teaspoons dry mustard

½ cup red wine vinegar

1 cup canola oil

Wash lettuce and pat dry with paper towels. Tear into bite-sized pieces. Mix lettuce and the remaining ingredients for salad in a large serving bowl.

Mix all ingredients for dressing in a blender or container you can shake to blend. Blend well. Just before serving, pour dressing over salad and toss to coat.

---

Makes 12 to 16 servings

# PUMPKIN SOUP

1 large onion, chopped
5 cups sliced mushrooms
½ cup butter
⅓ cup flour
8 cups chicken broth
2 cups canned pumpkin
2 cups whipping cream
1 tablespoon curry
salt and pepper to taste
Tabasco to taste

Sauté onion and mushrooms in butter in a large stockpot. Remove from heat and add flour, chicken broth, and pumpkin. Stir to combine and bring to a boil. Reduce heat and simmer for 20 minutes. Add whipping cream and curry. Season with salt, pepper, and Tabasco to taste.

Makes 6 servings

## CHICKEN AND SQUASH SOUP

2 to 3 chicken breasts
2 carrots, peeled and sliced, or
   2 cups baby carrots
1 small yellow onion, cut in half
¼ cup fresh parsley
2 stalks green onion

6 potatoes, peeled and
   quartered
1 large piece banana squash,
   quartered
salt and pepper to taste
2 14-ounce cans chicken broth

Put all ingredients in a large stockpot, except chicken broth. Put in enough water to cover. Bring to a boil. Reduce heat and simmer over low heat for 1 hour. Remove from heat. Remove chicken, onion, and squash. When cool enough to handle, cut chicken and onion into pieces and return to soup. Scrape squash from peel into soup. Discard peel. Add chicken broth and heat through again before serving.

Makes 12 servings

# TOMATO AND ARTICHOKE SOUP

1 large onion, finely chopped
4 tablespoons butter or
    margarine
1 garlic clove, minced
1 15-ounce can artichoke
    hearts, chopped

1 28-ounce can tomatoes,
    undrained and chopped
2 14-ounce cans chicken broth
½ teaspoon salt or to taste
¼ teaspoon pepper or to taste
sour cream or grated Parmesan
    cheese for garnish

In a large saucepan or stockpot, sauté onion in butter or margarine until soft. Add garlic and sauté another minute. Add artichoke hearts, tomatoes, chicken broth, salt, and pepper. Cover and simmer for 30 minutes to 1 hour. Pour soup into bowls and garnish each bowl with a dollop of sour cream or grated Parmesan cheese.

------------------------------------

Makes 8 servings

## Clam Chowder

¾ cup butter, melted

1 cup flour

1 cup peeled and diced potatoes

1 cup diced celery

1 cup diced onion

1 cup diced green bell pepper

1 cup diced leeks

¾ cup chopped canned clams

¾ tablespoon coarse ground black pepper

1½ tablespoons salt

¾ tablespoon whole thyme

6 bay leaves

1 teaspoon Tabasco

2 cups water

¾ cup bottled clam juice

2 quarts half-and-half

Preheat oven to 325 degrees. Combine melted butter and flour in an ovenproof container and bake for 30 minutes. In a large saucepan, combine potatoes, celery, onion, green bell pepper, leeks, clams, pepper, salt, thyme, bay leaves, Tabasco, water, and clam juice. Simmer until potatoes are thoroughly cooked. Stir butter-flour mixture into chowder. Mixture should be slightly less thick than cookie dough. Remove chowder from heat. Stir in half-and-half until blended. Heat to serving temperature, stirring occasionally. Serve immediately.

Makes 12 servings

## Sesame Fire Chicken

4 to 6 chicken breasts
1 tablespoon oil
⅓ cup soy sauce
¼ cup brown sugar
½ cup + 1 tablespoon water
1 tablespoon ketchup

¼ cup apple juice
¼ to ½ teaspoon cayenne pepper
1 garlic clove, minced
1 green onion, sliced
2 teaspoons sesame seeds
2 tablespoons cornstarch

In a skillet, brown chicken in oil. In a small bowl, mix together soy sauce, brown sugar, ½ cup water, ketchup, juice, cayenne pepper, garlic, and onion. Put browned chicken in glass baking pan and pour mixture over top. Cover with foil and bake at 350 degrees for 40 minutes.

Toast sesame seeds on a pie tin in a 350-degree oven for 10 minutes. Watch to be sure seeds don't burn.

When chicken is cooked, remove it from pan and drain liquid into a saucepan. In a small bowl, combine cornstarch and 1 tablespoon water until smooth. Add to saucepan and heat mixture over medium heat, stirring until thickened. Spoon sauce over chicken and sprinkle with toasted sesame seeds to serve.

------------------------------------------
Makes 4 to 6 servings

# RED POTATO SALAD

8 medium red potatoes

5 eggs, hardboiled

1 cup mayonnaise

1 teaspoon mustard

1 to 2 tablespoons lemon juice

salt and pepper to taste

¼ bunch parsley

2 green onions, sliced

Boil potatoes with skins on in salted water. When potatoes are cool enough to handle, remove skins. (You can
leave some on for color, if desired.) Chop into bite-sized
pieces. Chop cooled hardboiled eggs into small pieces
and add to potatoes. In a separate bowl, mix mayonnaise, mustard, lemon juice, salt, and pepper. Fold into
potato and egg mixture. Finely chop parsley; add along
with green onion to salad. Add more mayonnaise, salt,
and pepper as needed.

Makes 12 to 15 servings

# CRISPY WONTONS

1 pound ground beef or pork
salt and pepper
½ head cabbage, finely chopped
4 green onions, sliced

1 package square wonton
    wrappers
oil for deep-frying

Brown ground beef or pork in a skillet, breaking up meat into small pieces; drain. Season generously with salt and pepper. Add cabbage and onion and mix well.

On a work surface, assemble wontons by placing a heaping teaspoonful of the meat mixture in the center of one wonton. Dip your finger in a bowl of water and run it around the edge of the wonton, then fold the wonton wrapper over the meat mixture at an angle to form a triangle. Seal wrapper by pressing together moistened edges. Repeat process for remaining wrappers.

Heat oil in a deep skillet to medium-high. If oil is smoking, skillet is too hot. Deep-fry wontons, a few at a time, 1 to 2 minutes, or until golden brown and crispy. Remove with a slotted spoon and drain on paper towels.

Makes up to 48 wontons

# PAPAYA–AVOCADO–GRAPEFRUIT SALAD

For Dressing:

6 tablespoons fresh lime juice

2 tablespoons olive oil

salt and pepper to taste

For Salad:

4 ripe papayas

4 ruby red grapefruit

2 medium ripe avocados

6 red lettuce leaves

½ cup minced red onion

For dressing, whisk together lime juice and oil in a small nonmetal bowl. Season with salt and pepper.

For salad, cut papayas lengthwise and remove skin. Scoop out and discard seeds. Cut in slices. Remove skin and white pith from grapefruit. Hold grapefruit over the bowl with the dressing to catch juice, and cut sections from membrane. Halve, pit, peel, and slice avocado.

Put a red lettuce leaf on each serving plate. Arrange papaya, grapefruit, and avocado slices on lettuce leaf. Stir dressing again and drizzle over salad. Sprinkle with red onion. Serve immediately.

--------------------------------

Makes 12 servings

# GINGER STIR-FRY

2 tablespoons oil
fresh gingerroot
1 cup pea pods
2 carrots, peeled and sliced at an angle
1 white onion, cut into ½-inch pieces
1 cup bamboo shoots
1 cup sliced fresh mushrooms
2 tomatoes, cut into ½-inch pieces

In a wok or large skillet, heat oil on medium-high heat (below the smoking point). Cut two slices from the piece of gingerroot and fry briefly in the oil to infuse oil with ginger. Discard ginger slices. Add pea pods, carrots, onion, and bamboo shoots and stir-fry until crisp-tender. Add mushrooms and tomatoes the last 2 to 3 minutes of cooking. Serve immediately.

Makes 8 servings

*Serve with white rice.*

# POACHED SALMON

1 fillet fresh salmon (2 to 3 pounds)
1 small red onion
1 tablespoon olive oil
1 lemon
2 to 4 tablespoons capers
fresh dill for garnish

Preheat oven to 325 degrees. Place salmon in a poaching dish and fill the pan with ½ inch of water. Bake 20 to 30 minutes. While salmon is cooking, thinly slice the red onion and sauté it in oil. Cut the lemon in half; slice one half into thin slices.

When salmon is done, remove it from oven and transfer to a serving plate. Squeeze juice of the remaining lemon half over it. Garnish with lemon slices, sautéed red onion, capers, and dill.

--------------------------------

Makes 12 servings

*Serve with lemon wedges and Spinach Pomegranate Salad (see recipe on page 90).*

## Spinach Pomegranate Salad

1 package baby spinach
seeds of ½ pomegranate
4 tablespoons crumbled blue
    cheese

3 green onions, trimmed and
    sliced
Italian salad dressing

Wash spinach and pat dry with paper towels. Put in a large bowl. Add pomegranate seeds, blue cheese, and onions. Toss with your favorite Italian salad dressing and serve.

---

Makes 8 servings

## ✳ DESSERTS ✳

From fluffy cakes to sweetly decorated cookies and tangy lemon concoctions to rich chocolate combinations, nothing makes the perfect wedding shower as easily as the perfect dessert.

## APRICOT ICE CREAM

1 pint whipping cream

1 6-ounce can evaporated milk

juice of ½ lemon

juice of ½ orange

½ banana, mashed

1 cup sugar

1½ cups sweetened apricot
    nectar

Mix all ingredients together. Put in small ice cream maker and follow manufacturer's directions.

Makes 2 quarts ice cream

# SOUR CREAM CHEESECAKE

**For Crust:**

2 cups graham cracker crumbs

½ cup sugar

½ cup butter, melted

**For Filling:**

24 ounces (3 packages)
Philadelphia cream cheese,
at room temperature

1½ cups sugar

3 eggs

1 cup sour cream

1 teaspoon vanilla

1 tablespoon lemon juice

Preheat oven to 350 degrees. To make crust, in a medium bowl mix graham cracker crumbs, sugar, and butter together. Press into the bottom of a springform pan.

To make filling, in a large bowl cream together cream cheese and sugar. Mix in eggs one at a time. Add sour cream, vanilla, and lemon juice. Mix well until smooth. Pour mixture over crust and bake for 30 minutes. Remove from oven and put into refrigerator. Chill for at least 4 hours or overnight.

Makes 12 servings

# TRIPLE CHOCOLATE CAKE

1 package devil's food cake mix
   (without pudding in the mix)
1 small box instant chocolate
   pudding
2 cups sour cream
1 cup butter, melted

5 eggs
1 teaspoon almond extract
2 cups semisweet chocolate
   chips
powdered sugar

Preheat oven to 350 degrees. Grease and flour a Bundt cake pan and set aside.

Combine cake mix and dry pudding mix in a large bowl. Make a well in the center. Pour in sour cream, butter, eggs, and almond extract. Beat on low until blended. Scrape sides and beat on medium for 4 minutes. Batter will be very thick, like frosting. Stir in chocolate chips.

Spoon batter into cake pan. Bake 50 to 55 minutes or until knife inserted in the center comes out clean. Cool for 10 minutes, and then invert on serving plate. When cake is cool, dust with powdered sugar before serving.

Makes 16 servings

## SUGAR COOKIES

For Dough:

½ cup butter, softened

½ cup sugar

2 eggs

1 teaspoon vanilla

2½ cups flour, sifted

2 teaspoons baking powder

For Icing:

1 cup powdered sugar

2 teaspoons milk

2 teaspoons light corn syrup

¼ teaspoon almond extract

assorted food coloring

Cream together butter and sugar. Beat in eggs and vanilla. Add dry ingredients a little at a time until all is incorporated. Chill dough for 2 to 4 hours before rolling out.

Preheat oven to 375 degrees. Roll out dough on a lightly floured surface until it's ¼ inch thick. Cut into desired shapes with cookie cutters. Bake 7 to 12 minutes. Cool, ice, and decorate as desired.

To make icing, stir together powdered sugar and milk in a small bowl until smooth. Beat in corn syrup and almond extract until icing is smooth and glossy. If icing is too thick, add more corn syrup. Divide icing into separate bowls and add food coloring to each to desired intensity. You can dip your sugar cookies, paint them with a brush, or spread the icing using a butter knife.

Makes 2 dozen cookies

# HALF-HEARTED COOKIES

**For Dough:**

¾ cup sugar

1 cup butter, softened

3 ounces cream cheese, softened

1 egg

½ teaspoon peppermint extract

3 cups flour

**For Glaze:**

1½ cups semisweet chocolate chips

⅓ cup butter (plus a little more to thin chocolate if needed)

In a large mixing bowl, combine sugar, butter, cream cheese, egg, and peppermint extract. Beat until light and fluffy. Add flour; beat until well mixed. Wrap dough in wax paper, flattening it out to about 1 inch thick so that rolling is easier later. Refrigerate until firm, at least 2 hours.

Heat oven to 375 degrees. Roll out dough on a lightly floured surface until it's ¼ inch thick. Cut out dough with floured heart-shaped cookie cutter. Place cookies on an ungreased baking sheet and bake 7 to 10 minutes. Loosen cookies and let cool completely.

To make the glaze, melt chocolate chips and butter in a small, deep bowl in the microwave. Stir until smooth. Dip half of each heart cookie into chocolate. Place on a baking sheet lined with wax paper. Refrigerate until chocolate is firm. Store covered in refrigerator.

------------------------------------------------------

Makes about 8 dozen cookies

## BERRY COBBLER

### For Cobbler:

3 heaping cups frozen
unsweetened boysenberries or
blackberries

2 heaping cups frozen unsweetened raspberries

2 tablespoons cornstarch

¼ cup warm water

1 to 1½ cups sugar

### For Topping:

1½ cups flour

⅓ cup + ¼ cup sugar, divided

½ teaspoon salt

1 teaspoon baking powder

½ teaspoon baking soda

4 tablespoons cold unsalted
butter, cut in pieces

⅓ cup plain yogurt

¼ cup milk

½ teaspoon vanilla

For cobbler, thaw berries, reserving the juice. Place ¾ to 1 cup of the juice in a saucepan. Dissolve cornstarch in water and add to juice. Add sugar. Heat over medium heat until mixture boils, stirring constantly. Boil 1 to 2 minutes, until clear and slightly thickened. Stir in thawed berries and let stand while making topping.

For topping, stir together flour, ⅓ cup sugar, salt, baking powder, and baking soda. Cut in butter pieces with a pastry blender or butter knife until small crumbs form.

In a small bowl, stir together yogurt, milk, and vanilla. Make a well in the center of the flour mixture and pour in yogurt mixture; stir until moist. Knead with your hands until dough forms a soft ball and the sides of the bowl are clean. Knead 4 to 6 times more. Place on a sheet of floured wax paper. Pat dough into ½-inch-thick circle. Cut with round or heart-shaped cookie cutter.

Pour fruit into a 7 x 9-inch baking dish. Place biscuits on top. Brush with a little milk or cream and sprinkle with ¼ cup sugar. Bake at 350 degrees for 25 to 30 minutes. Cobbler will be quite tart.

Makes 6 servings

*Serve warm with whipped cream or vanilla ice cream.*

# Hello Dolly Cookies

1½ cups crushed graham cracker crumbs
½ cup flour
2 teaspoons baking powder
½ cup margarine, melted
1 can sweetened condensed milk
1 cup coconut
1 16-ounce bag semisweet chocolate chips
½ cup walnuts (optional)

Preheat oven to 375 degrees. Mix graham cracker crumbs, flour, baking powder, margarine, and sweetened condensed milk together. Stir in coconut, chocolate chips, and nuts if using. Drop by spoonfuls onto a baking sheet and bake for 8 to 10 minutes. Allow cookies to cool before serving.

------------------------------------------

Makes 2 dozen cookies

# BAKED APPLES

6 apples

⅓ cup brown sugar

⅓ cup chopped nuts

⅓ cup raisins

¼ cup oatmeal

¼ teaspoon cinnamon

⅛ teaspoon nutmeg

¼ cup butter or margarine,
  softened

2 teaspoons lemon juice

1 cup apple juice

ice cream or whipped cream for
  garnish

cinnamon sticks for garnish

Heat oven to 350 degrees. Core apples, being careful
not to break through bottoms of apples. In a small bowl,
mix brown sugar, nuts, raisins, oatmeal, cinnamon,
nutmeg, butter, and lemon juice. Using a spoon, fill
each apple with mixture.

Place apples in a shallow baking pan. Pour apple juice
around apples and bake 40 to 45 minutes, or until apples
are fork-tender. Serve warm with vanilla or cinnamon ice
cream or a dollop of whipped cream. Garnish with whole
cinnamon sticks.

Makes 6 servings

# Pumpkin Dessert

For Crust:

1 package yellow cake mix,
    reserve 1 cup

½ cup butter, melted

1 egg

For Filling:

1 15-ounce can pumpkin

1½ cups canned milk

1½ cups sugar

4 eggs

1 teaspoon salt

2 teaspoons cinnamon

1 teaspoon vanilla

1 teaspoon ginger

For Topping:

1 cup reserved cake mix

¼ cup sugar

1 teaspoon cinnamon

⅛ cup butter

Preheat oven to 350 degrees. To make crust, put cake mix in a medium bowl, reserving 1 cup. Add butter and egg. Mix and spread into a greased 9 x 13-inch pan.

To make filling, in a separate bowl beat together pumpkin, canned milk, sugar, and eggs. Add salt, cinnamon, vanilla, and ginger and mix well. Pour over top of crust.

To make topping, in another bowl mix together the reserved cake mix, sugar, cinnamon, and butter. Mix until crumbly. Sprinkle over top of pumpkin mixture. Bake 1 hour or until toothpick inserted in the center comes out clean.

Makes 12 servings

# BETTER-THAN-SEX CAKE

1 German chocolate cake mix
1 cup semisweet chocolate chips
caramel ice cream topping
1 can sweetened condensed milk
1 12-ounce container frozen whipped topping, thawed
3 Heath toffee bars, crushed

Preheat oven to 350 degrees. Grease and flour a
9 x 13-inch pan. Prepare cake according to package
directions; pour batter into prepared pan. Bake 10
minutes, and then sprinkle with chocolate chips.
Continue baking until cake is done.

While cake is still hot, poke holes in it with the handle
of a wooden spoon. Drizzle caramel topping and sweetened condensed milk over warm cake; let cool. Top with
whipped topping. Sprinkle with crushed candy bars.

Makes 12 servings

**NOTE:** If this cake is too sweet for you, eliminate the sweetened
condensed milk.

# LAYERED COCONUT CAKE

1 package white cake mix
1 small box vanilla pudding (cooked not instant)
1 12-ounce container frozen whipped topping, thawed
1 7-ounce package coconut
1 to 2 cups fresh berries (optional)

Grease and flour two 8-inch round cake pans. Make cake according to package directions. Make pudding according to package directions. When cake is completely cool, place one layer on a serving plate. Top with pudding. Spread evenly, leaving about ½-inch border around the edge of the cake with no pudding. Gently place the second layer of cake on top and press down very lightly to set the layers together. Frost top and sides of cake with whipped topping. Sprinkle top and sides with coconut. Garnish with fresh berries, if desired.

Makes 12 servings

# Black-Bottom Banana Cream Pie

For Crust:

2 cups boxed Oreo
cookie crumbs

½ cup sugar
½ cup margarine, melted

For Filling:

1 large box banana pudding mix
(cooked not instant)

For Topping:

1 pint sweetened whipping
cream

sliced bananas for garnish
fresh mint sprigs for garnish

For piecrust, mix together cookie crumbs, sugar, and margarine. Press into the bottom of a pie pan.

Make pudding according to package directions. Pour into Oreo piecrust. Cover with wax paper and cool in the refrigerator for at least 4 hours.

To serve, slice pie and top each slice with a dollop of whipped cream, 3 slices of banana, and a sprig of mint.

------------------------------------

Makes 8 servings

# Fresh Raspberry Pie

2 refrigerated piecrusts*
2 tablespoons butter or margarine
3 cups fresh raspberries
1 cup sugar
2 tablespoons instant tapioca

Preheat oven to 350 degrees. Fit bottom piecrust into pie pan. Prick holes in it with a fork and dot with butter. Spread raspberries evenly on crust. Sprinkle evenly with sugar. Sprinkle tapioca evenly over top. Cut second piecrust into 1½-inch-thick strips. Weave over the top of pie to make a lattice piecrust. Bake for 30 to 40 minutes.

-----------------------------------

Makes 8 servings

*If you have a favorite piecrust recipe, you can substitute it.*

# TRIFLE

1 angel food cake
1 small box vanilla pudding (cooked not instant)
2 cups combination of sliced strawberries, blueberries, and
  boysenberries
1 cup sweetened whipping cream
¼ to ½ cup sliced almonds

Make angel food cake according to package directions
or purchase cake made. Cut cake in ¾-inch cubes.
Place half the cubes in the bottom of a large, clear
glass bowl. Prepare pudding according to package directions. Spoon half of pudding on top of cake cubes.
Arrange half of fruit on top of pudding. Repeat with a
second layer of cake cubes, pudding, and fruit. Top with
whipped cream. Cover and refrigerate until thoroughly
chilled, at least 1 hour. Just before serving, top with
sliced almonds.

Makes 10 servings

# FROZEN LEMONADE DESSERT

**For Crust:**

2 cups Ritz cracker crumbs

½ cup margarine, melted

¼ cup powdered sugar

**For Filling:**

1 6-ounce can frozen lemonade

1 can sweetened condensed milk

1 8-ounce container frozen whipped topping, thawed

fresh mint sprigs for garnish

For crust, mix cracker crumbs, margarine, and powdered sugar together. Press three-fourths of the mixture into the bottom of a 9 x 13-inch pan, reserving the rest.

For filling, in a medium-sized bowl beat lemonade, condensed milk, and whipped topping together. Pour over crust; top with reserved crumb mixture. Freeze for up to 4 hours before serving. Cut into squares and garnish with sprigs of mint.

Makes 12 servings

## For an Easy Fix

*When you don't have much time but would still like to serve a beautiful dessert plate, try the following:*

- *Miniature cream puffs (available in the frozen section of most grocery stores). Drizzle one plate of cream puffs with chocolate syrup and sprinkle another plate of cream puffs with powdered sugar.*

- *Lu the Little Schoolboy cookies. Buy hazelnut and dark chocolate cookies. Arrange on a plate alternating the light and dark cookies.*

- *Bowl of fresh strawberries (wash but leave the green tops on).*

- *Entenmann's key lime pie. Top each slice with a dollop of fresh whipped cream and a fresh strawberry slice.*

- *Mrs. Smith's french apple pie. Bake according to package directions. Serve warm with a scoop of vanilla bean ice cream.*

# ✳ DRINKS ✳

These refreshing drinks make a nice addition to many of the lunch and brunch recipes included earlier.

## FRESH LIMEADE

9 quarters fresh lime
8 cups water
2 tablespoons sweetened condensed milk
2 cups sugar

Put quarters of lime, including peel, in a juicer. Combine lime juice, water, sweetened condensed milk, and sugar. Mix thoroughly and refrigerate at least 2 hours. Serve with lots of ice.

----

Makes 10 servings

## CRANBERRY PUNCH

1 quart cranberry juice
1 quart apple juice
1 2-liter bottle lemon-lime soda

Chill juices and soda before combining. Mix all together and serve in glasses over crushed ice. Or freeze until slushy and serve.

--------------------------------
Makes 24 servings

## ORANGE-PINEAPPLE PUNCH

4 cups pineapple juice
2 cups orange juice
1 cup coconut milk
crushed ice

Mix all ingredients together and pour into chilled glasses.

Makes 8 servings

## Sweetheart Champagne

4 ounces lemon vodka, chilled
16 ounces champagne
4 dashes grenadine

Pour 1 ounce of vodka into each of 4 chilled champagne flutes, and then fill each flute with 4 ounces champagne. Add a dash of grenadine to each drink.

------------------------------------

Makes 4 servings

# PASSION FRUIT DAIQUIRI

2 ounces simple syrup
6 ounces light rum
2 ounces lime juice
2 ounces passion fruit juice
crushed ice

Make simple syrup ahead by mixing 1 cup of sugar with 1 cup of water in a medium saucepan and bringing to a boil; boil for 5 minutes. Keep covered in the refrigerator.

To make daiquiris, mix simple syrup, rum, lime juice, and passion fruit juice together in a blender with crushed ice. Strain into chilled cocktail glasses.

--------------------------------

Makes 4 servings

# FAVORS

Favors are such a simple thing to do, and they make the shower much more memorable. It's fun to send your guests off with their own memento from the party. You can use certain favors as part of your decorations or center-pieces, and then send them home with your guests. If you want to give a gift that is a little more expensive, you can buy one nicer gift and then make it a prize for a game or have everyone enter a drawing for it. Or you can stick with something a little more simple and affordable for each guest.

The trick to making favors special is all in the presen-tation. Wrap them in creative boxes or containers, use beautiful paper, fun nametags, and different ribbons. With the right presentation, even a two-dollar lip balm can feel like the perfect gift. Here are some fun ideas for favors.

It's almost a universal truth that women love to get flowers—whether they're from a lover, a husband, a girlfriend, or even as a wedding shower favor. Be creative in using flowers, bulbs, plants, and herbs. They make great party favors.

Use a bouquet of long-stemmed roses as a centerpiece. At the end of the shower, let each woman take a rose home with her.

Buy small glass or silver bud vases—they often come in packs of three. Fill them with tiny, unusual flowers to make beautiful miniature bouquets. Sweet peas, cornflowers, coffee beans, lilies of the valley, and tiny orchids are just some of the flowers that work well in this kind of arrangement.

Arrange a gerbera daisy or other bloom in a small bud vase. Cut the stem only an inch or two from the bud and let the bloom fill the entire vase.

Tie fresh lavender bunches with ribbon and give as a fragrant favor. Or fill sachets with dried lavender.

Plant small terra-cotta pots with your favorite annual or a flower to match the bride's colors. These can be clustered nicely as centerpieces or decorations for a gift table so guests can enjoy them throughout the shower before they take theirs home.

Give fresh potted herbs. In a small pot, miniature

## Packaging TIPS

*Confectionaries, craft stores, and many paper supply stores have small gift boxes that are the perfect size for favors. They can be dressed up with wrapping paper, fabric, ribbon, scrapbooking paper, lace, craft paper, or even wallpaper pieces. The presentation of your favors should rival the tiny memento inside.*

galvanized tin bucket, window box, or other creative container, plant a fragrant fresh herb, such as rosemary, lavender, mint, sage, or lemon verbena.

For a Christmas shower, buy fresh mistletoe. Tie small bundles with red ribbon and give away.

Place fresh rose petals in small boxes. Though completely impractical, there is something so luxuriant about them. Tie each box with an elegant, thick silk ribbon.

Pot an amaryllis bulb or paperwhites. These are great gifts for the wintertime and will remind your guests of the good time they had at the shower when the flowers bloom in the spring.

Buy simple ivy topiaries for each guest or a more expensive one as a centerpiece to give away as a prize. To dress it up, tie the topiary with netting ribbon matching the shower's colors.

## ◦ RICH AND LUSCIOUS ◦

We've all heard that when women eat chocolate it produces the same chemical reaction as falling in love. Whether you believe that's true or not, it's hard to go wrong offering chocolate as a wedding shower favor. Give one of the following.

- Small box of four chocolates wrapped in gold or silver foil and tied with gold or silver ribbon.
- European chocolate, such as Toblerone or Lindt bars. These can be found in any grocery store. Toblerones are especially fun to wrap because of the triangle-shaped box.
- Bunches of chocolate mints with pastel candy coating placed in netting and tied with ribbon. These are a traditional candy for weddings and showers.
- Boxed sandwich mints.
- Chocolate kisses. You can mix the almond kisses and the plain ones. Tie in cellophane for a simple favor with a hint of romance.
- Chocolate-dipped pretzels.
- Chocolate-dipped strawberries or clusters of chocolate-dipped raspberries.

## ○ FORGET ME NOT ○

Small keepsakes are often the most treasured wedding shower favors. Many are simple to make or inexpensive to buy, yet they add that touch of thoughtfulness that says you were thinking of your guests.

Candles come in all shapes and sizes. They can be scented or unscented, filled with pressed leaves or flowers, or housed in fun containers. The candles I've found with the best-lasting scents are Salt City Candles and Votivo, Ltd.

Handmade bookmarks are a personalized favor. You can write a quotation, a love poem, or an inside joke among friends—something to remind your guests of the shower or of your friendship. You can also buy nice bookmarks at Barnes & Noble and other bookstores and gift shops.

Christmas ornaments are a great shower gift for December. A clear glass bowl filled with ornaments makes a lovely centerpiece for your table, and then guests can each select one to take home.

Picture frames are always a favorite. Guests can use their frames for a photo from the wedding, a favorite photo of friends, or even a fun snapshot from the shower itself.

Bath gels or salts make personal gifts that encourage guests to pamper themselves.

Fragrant room sprays are a nice party favor. Just make

sure none of your guests are sensitive to perfumes or fragrances.

A lingerie sachet can be an elegant little gift. This is an especially nice favor to give at a lingerie shower.

Lip balm or gloss is a simple favor most guests will appreciate. (Burt's Bees beeswax lip balm is great.) This can be dressed up as a shower favor if it's wrapped well, or placed in a package with several small favors.

Funky magnets are always fun. Mighty Magnets from Lucy Lu Designs is a great brand, and there are many others as well. You can buy a set of magnets and divide them up or you can buy individual letter magnets for the first name of each of your guests. Wrap them individually with cellophane and put them in a mini gift bag along with a scented soap, individually wrapped chocolates, and/or other small gifts.

Handwritten love poems or quotations, rolled up and tied with ribbon, make a romantic take-home gift. Place them in a small basket and let guests take one as they leave the shower.

## GREAT QUOTATIONS ON LOVE

"Let me not to the marriage of true minds
        Admit impediments. Love is not love
Which alters when it alteration finds,
        Or bends with the remover to remove:
O no! it is an ever-fixed mark
        That looks on tempests and is never shaken."
                            —from Shakespeare's Sonnet 116

"The best and most beautiful things in the world cannot be seen, or even touched. They must be felt in the heart." —Helen Keller

"Grow old along with me, the best is yet to be!"
                            —Robert Browning

"The greatest thing you'll ever learn is just to love and be loved in return." —from Moulin Rouge

"Love demands everything, and rightly so." —Ludwig van Beethoven

"If I could measure the beauty of her eyes, I was born to look in them and know myself." —from Shakespeare in Love

"If there is anything better than to be loved, it is loving."
                            —Anonymous

# DETAILS

When it comes to entertaining, it's surprising how much is dependent on the details. Whether it is a garnish on a dessert plate or a tiny metal wedding bell tied to the ribbon of a package, the details are what make a shower really stand out. Find clever or unusual shower invitations, use interesting greenery in your floral centerpieces, wrap your packages creatively, and search out that perfect little gift for the favors to make your shower something special. The details will make the difference between an average party and something to be remembered.

Following are a few suggestions for details you can incorporate into your wedding shower:

- Always use real flowers.
- Line wrapping paper with a layer of tissue paper.
- Use china or pottery, glass glasses, and real flat-ware. Steer away from paper plates and plastic flatware.
- Use a punch bowl.
- Find a little trinket or sprig of something—such as an ornament, a button, a fresh flower, or a sprig of rosemary—to tie to the ribbon on packages.
- Stand up silverware in a small pottery container instead of laying it on the table, or wrap it in cloth napkins so guests can pick up the entire bundle.
- Freeze raspberries in ice cubes for your punch.
- Tie ribbons around bars of soap for shower favors, around a place card, or around the napkins.
- Handwrite the addresses on your invitations—don't use labels. Choose love stamps or stamps that match your shower's theme.
- Serve food in striking dishes, like soup in a small hollowed-out pumpkin, or fruit salad in a coconut half.

- Incorporate holidays when you can. Give shower favors in small, stylized stockings at Christmastime or sprinkle your buffet table with heart-shaped confetti at Valentine's.
- Write out the directions to your house and include them with your invitation. This is more attractive than including a xeroxed map. Give directions to the guests without their having to ask.

## ∘ IN CONCLUSION ∘

The shower you give will be one of the events the bride remembers all of her life as part of her wedding celebration. Enjoy the planning and enjoy the event. Be creative as you celebrate your friendship and the future with those you love.

TIP: Enjoy the planning and enjoy the event.

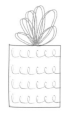

## About the Author

**Jennifer Adams** received her degree in English from the University of Washington in Seattle. She lives and works in Salt Lake City as a writer and editor. Jennifer enjoys good literature, good friends, and good chocolate. She has hosted dozens of parties and showers for friends, coworkers, neighbors, and family members. She is also the author of *Lion House Weddings* and *Baby Showers,* and the coauthor of *Packing Up a Picnic.*